male

2.75–4"

2.5–4.2"

Pipevine Swallowtail
black overall; males have greenish blue iridescent hindwing; fast, low flight; distasteful to many predators

Black Swallowtail
black with yellow spot bands, eye-spot with central black pupil near tail; common in gardens; larvae feed on dill, fennel and other plants

female

3.5–5.5"

male

3.5–5"

Eastern Tiger Swallowtail
mostly black with faint, darker black stripes; hindwing with blue scaling and tail; largest butterfly in the Midwest

Spicebush Swallowtail
pale green spots on wing margins, pronounced greenish blue scaling; orange eyespot and tail; regularly puddle at moist ground

3–3.5"

1.75–2.5"

White Admiral
broad white spot band across both wings, hindwing with outer band of red spots

Baltimore Checkerspot
rows of small white spots, large reddish orange marginal spots; found in wetlands; declining across the region

3–4"

1.75–2.5"

Mourning Cloak
broad irregular yellow wing borders; outer row of purple-blue spots; adults overwinter; often the first butterfly seen in spring

Red Admiral
forewing with central reddish band, white apical spots; hindwing with broad red border

male   2.8–3.75"

Common Sootywing
shiny black; forewing and head with white spots

Promethea Silkmoth
brownish black, tan wing borders, forewing apex with pink around single dark eyespot; males fly during late afternoon

4.9–5.9"

1.8–2.2"

Cecropia Silkmoth
abdomen has white stripes; adult wingspan often approaches 6"; large green larvae have red and yellow tubercles

Virgin Tiger Moth
forewing black with cream lines; hindwing and abdomen pink to yellow with black spots

1–1.5"

Eight-spotted Forester
forewing with two yellow spots; hindwing with two white spots; adults fly during the day

male

0.75–1"

Eastern Tailed-Blue
the only blue with hindwing tails; females brownish gray above; often common to abundant; males often feed at mud puddles

0.75–1"

Spring Azure
dusky blue with black spots and dark scaling along margin; found in early spring; larvae feed on dogwood, cherry and viburnum blooms

0.8–1.25"

Summer Azure
chalky blue with faint dark spots

1–1.25"

Silvery Blue
dull gray with band of round white-outlined black spots; often local and uncommon

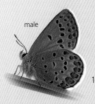

male

1–1.25"

Karner Blue
unmarked bright blue above; whitish gray below with orange submarginal band; endangered; larvae feed on wild lupine

female

3.5–4.4"

Diana Fritillary
black basally with iridescent blue spots on outer half; females mimic toxic Pipevine Swallowtail; adults fond of milkweed and Joe Pye weed blossoms

3–4"

Red-spotted Purple
forewing jet black; hindwing with iridescent blue scaling; mimics toxic Pipevine Swallowtail; adults feed on sap, rotting fruit and dung

4.5–5.5"

Giant Swallowtail
broad yellow spot bands; hindwing tail with yellow center; larvae resemble bird droppings; adults continuously flutter wings while feeding

0.9–1.2"

Henry's Elfin
hindwing with two-toned pattern; gray frosting along margin; short tail

0.9–1.25"

Coral Hairstreak
gray-brown; hindwing with coral spot band along margin; tailless; adults fond of milkweed blossoms

1–1.25"

Edwards' Hairstreak
gray-brown wings with white-rimmed black spots

1–1.25"

Banded Hairstreak
band of dark dashes edged outwardly in white; hair-like tails resemble antennae and help deflect attacking predators

1–1.25"

Hickory Hairstreak
dark dashes edged in white on both sides

0.75–1"

Red-banded Hairstreak
broad red band edged outwardly in white; larvae feed on dead leaves and plant material below their host

1–1.3"

Striped Hairstreak
wide, dark bands outlined in white; uncommon and highly localized

1–1.5"

White-M Hairstreak
hindwing with a white band forming an "M" near red patch

female

1–1.25"

Melissa Blue
male bright blue; female primarily brown; hindwing with row of orange-capped black spots; found in western portions of region

1.6–1.9"

American Snout
forewing with orange basal scaling; named for its snout-like mouthparts; resembles a dead leaf; adults have quick, bouncy flight

2–2.6"

Hackberry Emperor
triangular wings; forewing apex black with white spots and black eyespot; males investigate passing organisms, including people

2–2.75"

Tawny Emperor
triangular wings; forewing apex black without white spots

1.4–2"

Silvery Checkerspot
tawny orange with black markings and borders; hindwing with white in center of black spots

1.1–1.4"

Gorgone Checkerspot
orange with black markings; hindwing with row of solid black spots

1.4–1.9"

Pearl Crescent
orange with black bands, spots and borders; widespread and common; larvae feed on asters

1.6–2.7"

Common Buckeye
conspicuous eyespots; forewing with broad white band; often perch on bare ground; wary and difficult to approach

2.5–3.1"

Compton Tortoiseshell
irregular wing margins; forewing apex squared off; hindwing with white spot and stubby tail; common in northern part of our region

1.75–2.6"

Northern Pearly-eye
violet cast, row of yellow-rimmed dark eyespots; adults often active on cloudy days; does not visit flowers

1.6–2.25"

Eyed Brown
jagged dark line through wings, row of yellow-rimmed dark eyespots; found in wetlands; adults have slow, bouncing flight

1.1–1.5"

Common Ringlet
forewing with black eyespot near apex; hindwing two-toned with pale wavy central band

1.5–1.9"

Little Wood-Satyr
two dark lines on wings; wings with two large yellow-rimmed eyespots; often common; adults perch with wings partially open

1.8–2.8"

Common Wood-Nymph
variable eyespot border; may have yellow forewing patch; generally common; open grasslands, prairies, wet meadows; adults visit flowers

1.75–2.4"

Silver-spotted Skipper
elongated forewing; hindwing with large white patch; largest, showiest skipper in region; larvae construct leaf shelters

1.4–1.75"

Hoary Edge
hindwing with hoary white marginal patch

1.2–1.7"

Northern Cloudywing
forewing with small misaligned white spots

1.2–1.6"

Southern Cloudywing
forewing with prominent band of aligned glassy spots

1–1.4"

Hayhurst's Scallopwing
checkered fringe; hindwing with scalloped margin

1–1.6"

Dreamy Duskywing
forewing lacks glassy spots

1.5–1.9"

Juvenal's Duskywing
forewing with extensive gray scaling and glassy cell end spot; common to abundant in early spring

1.25–1.75"

Horace's Duskywing
forewing with less extensive gray scaling and usually lacks glassy cell end spot

female

1–1.25"

Fiery Skipper
hindwing orange-brown with several scattered dark spots; temporary colonist; found in disturbed areas; very fond of flowers

female

1–1.6"

Sachem
hindwing with angled pale spot band or patch

1–1.25"

Peck's Skipper
hindwing with two broad yellow spot bands

0.8–1.25"

Tawny-edged Skipper
forewing with orange scaling along costal margin; hindwing unmarked

female

1–1.4"

Zabulon Skipper
lavender-gray scaling along outer wing margins; hindwing with white bar along apex

1–1.4"

Mulberry Wing
hindwing with yellow spot band bisected by long central ray

0.8–1.25"

Arctic Skipper
dark brown dorsally with orange spots; hindwing below yellow-orange with dark rimmed pale spots

0.8–1.1"

Brown Elfin
hindwing two-toned appearance and lobed anal angle

1–1.3"

Common Roadside-Skipper
forewing with white apical spots; hindwing dark with violet gray scaling on outer half

female

1–1.3"

Io Moth
forewing reddish brown; hindwing with large black eyespot and broad pink anal margin

4–5.8"

Polyphemus Moth
hindwing with dark band; males have broad ferny antennae; eyespots may startle predators or deflect attacks from body

female

3–4"

Promethea Silkmoth
wings two-toned pink-brown with dark bases and pale central line; female flies at night

2.4–3.6"

White-lined Sphinx
forewing with wide diagonal white line from apex; hindwing with pink center; feeds like a hummingbird at flowers; active at dusk and dawn

1.7–3.25"

Twin-spotted Sphinx
forewing with irregular outer margin; hindwing with pink center and large dark eyespot

2–2.8"

Abbott's Sphinx
forewing with bark-like pattern and irregular outer margin; hindwing yellow basally; adults buzz in flight; larvae have large eyespot on rear end

1.5–2.2"

Hummingbird Clearwing
narrow transparent wings with reddish brown borders, thorax olive, abdomen blackish; common daytime flower visitor

1.8–2.9"

Walnut Sphinx
variable bark-like pattern, outer margin of wings somewhat scalloped; larvae feed on walnut and hickory; adults do not feed

Eastern Tent Caterpillar Moth

forewing with two white central lines; larvae form large silk webs on trees in spring; minor forest pest

0.9–1.4"

Banded Tussock Moth

forewing with dark-outlined spot bands and pointed apex; hairs on larvae can irritate skin; also called Pale Tiger Moth

1.5–1.75"

Darling Underwing

forewing dark gray-brown with green scaling; hindwing banded pink and black with pale margins

1.8–2.1"

Curved-toothed Geometer

wings mottled yellow-brown; forewing with dark line leading along apex

1.5–2.2"

Gray Copper
wings dark gray; hindwing with orange band along margin; uncommon to rare in many parts of range

Acadian Hairstreak
postmedian band or black spots outlined in white, hindwing with orange-capped blue patch; in wetlands; adults fond of milkweeds

Gray Hairstreak
wings uniformly gray with narrow black and white line; hindwing with orange-capped black spot; arguably most common hairstreak in region

Common Checkered-Skipper
black with white spots and dashes; wing fringes checkered

Modest Sphinx
forewing gray-brown with pale gray base; hindwing crimson with dark crescent-shaped eyespot

The Penitent Underwing
forewing gray and brown in bark-like pattern; hindwing banded orange and black with pale margin

White-marked Tussock Moth
forewing gray with rounded apex and pale spot near anal angle

Pink-spotted Hawkmoth
forewing gray-brown in bark-like pattern; hindwing with pink basal spot, abdomen striped pink and black

0.8–1.1"

3–4.2"

Juniper Hairstreak
olive green with white spot band; always found near stands of Eastern Redcedar trees

Luna Moth
pale green, each wing with single eyespot, hindwing with long curved tail; often found at lights; long tail helps thwart bat attacks

3.3–4.5"

0.5–0.9"

Pandorus Sphinx
forewing green with dark olive markings and pink streaks

Wavy-lined Emerald
emerald green with thin, pale wavy lines

1.1–2"

Pale Beauty
pale green with two dark-outlined pale lines; hindwing margin irregular with stubby tail

1.3–2"

Sleepy Orange
hindwing butter yellow with brown markings; appears orange in flight

1.1–1.3"

Harvester
only butterfly with carnivorous larvae; rarely visits flowers; found in small, localized colonies

0.9–1.4"

American Copper
forewing orange with dark spots and margins; hindwing with wavy orange band; can be very abundant

1.25–1.65"

Bronze Copper
forewing orange; hindwing gray with dark spots and orange marginal band

3.5–4"

Monarch
orange with black veins and borders; forewing with white apical spots; can migrate thousands of miles; larvae feed on milkweed

1.75–2.3"

Variegated Fritillary
forewing somewhat elongated; wings with light central band and darker orange basally

male

3.5–4.5"

Diana Fritillary
wings unmarked blackish brown with broad orange margins; found in southern portions of region; males and females dimorphic

2.9–3.8"

Great Spangled Fritillary
bright orange with black lines and spots; wings dark basally; common; adults very fond of flowers

2.7–3.3"

Aphrodite Fritillary
bright orange with black lines and spots, wings dark basally; forewing with dark basal spot along inner margin

3.1–4"

Regal Fritillary
hindwing with white postmedian spots; restricted to prairie remnants; rare and declining; adults fond of milkweeds and thistles

1.6–2.3"

Silver-bordered Fritillary
orange with black borders enclosing orange spots; forewing apex rounded

1.25–1.9"

Meadow Fritillary
forewing elongated with squared off apex; wings dark basally

2.6–3.3"

Viceroy
orange with black veins and borders; hindwing with postmedian black line; resembles the Monarch; typically found near wetlands

2.25–3"

Question Mark
forewing with jagged margins; named for silver question mark spot on underside; adults feed on dung, fruit sap and rotting fruit

2–2.4"

Eastern Comma
forewing apex squared off; margins irregular and jagged; hindwing with stubby tail

1.9–2.4"

Milbert's Tortoiseshell
wings dark with wide yellow orange band; forewing with two orange bars, margins irregular and jagged

1.75–2.4"

Painted Lady
pinkish orange with dark marks; forewing black with white spots

1.75–2.4"

American Lady
forewing with small white spot in orange field; common in open disturbed sites; larvae construct silken shelters on host

2.25–3"

Goatweed Leafwing
forewing with hooked apex, hindwing with tail; wings have dead leaf pattern below; fast, erratic flight; wary and difficult to approach

0.7–1"

Least Skipper
forewing dark with orange border; hindwing unmarked orange; small; adults have low, weak flight; males have long pointed abdomens

0.9–1.1"

European Skipper
bronzy orange with dark borders; veins darkened toward margins; non-native, from Europe; fond of flowers; common garden butterfly

male

0.9–1.1"

Fiery Skipper
hindwing orange with scattered black spots

male

1.5–1.75"

Sachem
hindwing golden brown with angled pale spot band or patch

1.5–1.75"

Leonard's Skipper
hindwing reddish brown with cream-white spot band; adults have strong, powerful flight; occurs in late summer through early fall

Mostly orange

Delaware Skipper
wings unmarked golden orange
1–1.4"

Hobomok Skipper
hindwing purplish brown with broad yellow-orange central patch; females have two forms
1.4–1.6"

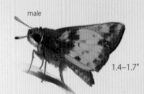

male

Zabulon Skipper
hindwing yellow with dark base enclosing yellow spot
1.4–1.7"

Dion Skipper
hindwing tawny orange with pale central ray
1.4–1.7"

Painted Lichen Moth
adults are distasteful to predators and make ultrasonic noises to warn bats about unpalatability; larvae eat algae and lichen on trees
1–1.4"

Royal Walnut Moth
forewing grayish with orange veins and yellow spots; hindwing orange; large, spiny larvae are called Hickory Horned Devils
3.9–6"

Mostly white

Zebra Swallowtail
white and black striped; hindwing with red eyespot and long tail; found in southern parts of the region; not common in urban areas
2.5–4"

Mostly white

male

1.25–1.75"

Falcate Orangetip
forewing with hooked apex; orange tip and single black eyespot; single spring generation

male

1.25–2"

Cabbage White
forewing black-tipped and black eyespot (male), two eyespots (female); non-native; garden pest of cabbage, broccoli and cauliflower

1.25–2"

Checkered White
white and black checkered pattern; dark scaling is seasonally variable; found in open, disturbed areas

1.25–2.2"

Mustard White
unmarked white to smoky white; forewing with rounded apex

1.25–1.75"

Olympia Marble
hindwing white with yellow-green marbling; fresh individuals with pink flush near wing base

2.4–3.5"

Great Leopard Moth
forewing and thorax white with black circles and spots, abdomen black; larvae curl up in a ball when disturbed

1.1–1.5"

Delicate Cycnia
wings unmarked pure white; forewing with pale yellow leading margin

0.65–0.8"

Common Spring Moth
white with broad black borders; forewing apex black with partial white band

Mostly yellow

3.5–5.5"

Eastern Tiger Swallowtail

large, wide black stripes; broad black wing margin; hindwing with single tail (yellow-form male and female)

1.9–2.3"

Clouded Sulphur

yellow to greenish yellow below, pink wing fringes; hindwing with large red-rimmed silver spot; common in clover and alfalfa fields

1.9–2.3"

Orange Sulphur

hindwing with red-rimmed spot and dark spot band; common in clover and alfalfa; often appears orange in flight; some females white

2–2.6"

Southern Dogface

forewing with black cell spot; named for the dog head profile on upper surface of forewing; only sulphur with a pointed forewing

2.25–3"

Cloudless Sulphur

large, greenish yellow with limited dark spots; hindwing with small central silver spot; largest sulphur in the region; migrates south in fall

1–1.6"

Little Yellow

small, yellow to near white, several dark spots or patches; seasonal colonist in the region; low, erratic flight

0.75–1.25"

Dainty Sulphur

elongated wings; forewing with orange scaling along leading edge and few black spots; smallest sulphur in the region

male

2–3.2"

Io Moth

hindwing with a large dark eye-spot and broad pink anal margin; larvae have venomous spines that can inflict a painful sting